This book belongs to

ISBN 0 7239 0089 2

© Oyster Books Ltd 1995
Rhymes © Jenny Wood and Ali Brooks 1992

Grateful thanks are due to Lizzy Pearl for her assistance
during the early stages of this book's development.

Printed and bound in Italy

MY BIG BEAR BOOK

Words by Jenny Wood
Illustrations by Rebecca Archer

My name is Big Bear.
These are all my friends.
Turn the page to find out
their names.

What is your name?
Do you have a bear?
What is your bear called?

Say hello to the Bears.

Can you remember the name of
the bear who is lifting the weights?

The Bears want to paint pictures.
Big Bear is telling them the names
of all the colours they can use.
Try to say the names of all the colours.
Which is your favourite colour?

red

purple brown

yellow   blue   green   orange

black   white   grey

The Bears are having a busy day.
Some of the Bears are painting their house.
Some of the Bears are painting the garden fence.
What is Yellow Bear doing?
What colour is Big Bear painting the gate?
Point to all the green things you can see in the picture.

The Bears are learning to count.
Try to count with them. Say the numbers out loud.

1
one
drum

2
two balls

How many bears are playing a drum?
Which number comes after **1**?
How many bears are trying on hats?
How many books can you see?

3 three hats

4 four books

5
five jumps

6
six fish

7
seven bikes

How many bears
are jumping?

How many fish
can you see?

What colour is
White Bear's bike?

Which number
comes after 7?

8
eight
umbrellas

9
nine sledges

10

10
ten kites

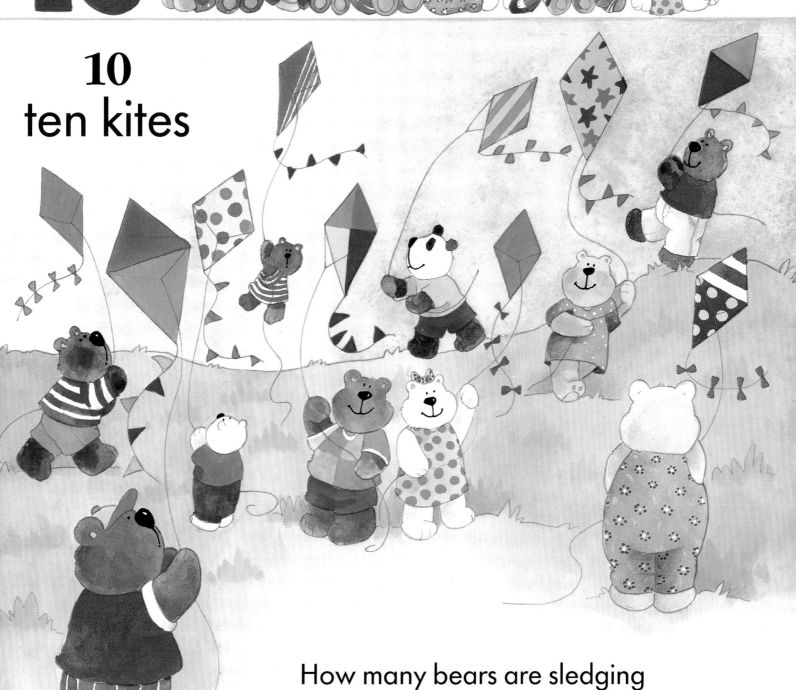

How many bears are sledging down the hill?
How many kites can you see?
Can you point to the blue kites?

1 one
·

2 two
··

3 three
···

4 four
····

5 five
·····

How many bears are playing with the ball?
What colour are the swings?
How many bears are in the sandpit?
Can you point to the number 5?
Can you remember all the numbers from 1 to 10?

6
six
. . . . . .

7
seven
. . . .

8
eight
. . . . .
. . .

9
nine
. . . . .
. . . .

10
ten
. . . . .
. . . . .

The Bears are learning about shapes.
Shapes have names. Try to say the names out loud.

This shape is called a **circle**.

This shape is called a **square**.

This shape is called a **triangle**.

Which shape is Big Bear pushing?
What colour is the square?
Can you point to the triangle?
Can you see any other
triangles on the page?

This shape is called an **oblong**.

What colour is the oblong?

Can you see any other oblongs on the page?

This shape is called a **diamond**.

This shape is called a **star**.

Can you point to the diamond?
Which shape is Orange Bear holding?
How many stars can you see on the page?

What shape is Yellow Bear's kite?
Can you see a circle in the picture?
Can you see a square in the picture?
How many bears are in the boat?
What colour is the boat's sail?
Can you remember the names of all the shapes?

circle

square

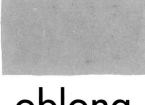

triangle

oblong

diamond

star

big

The Bears are learning that
everything has a size.
Big Bear is **big**.
Small Bear is **little**.

Some things are **tiny**.
Brown Bear and Panda Bear
have found a tiny insect.

little

tiny

Grey Bear is standing on stilts.
The stilts make her very **tall**.

Orange Bear's trousers are **long**.
Black Bear's trousers are **short**.

tall

long

short

The Bears are learning that some things go together.
Here are some that you might know.

soap and flannel

toothbrush and toothpaste

vest and pants

hat and coat

Try to say the words out loud.

paint and paintbrush

bowl and spoon

bat and ball

bucket and spade

Can you think of any other things that go together?

The Bears do different things at different times of the day.
Early in the morning, the Bears eat breakfast.

What do you like to eat for breakfast?

After breakfast, the Bears play with their toys.

What is Tiny Bear doing?
Which of your toys do you like best?

Before the Bears go to bed, they have a bath.
They love the warm water.

Do you like having a bath?

After their bath, it is time for
the Bears to go to bed.
Big Bear reads a bedtime story.
But White Bear has fallen asleep.
What is your favourite bedtime story?

The Bears are learning that each part of the body
has its own name.
Do you know the names of the parts of the body
White Bear is pointing to?

eyes

nose

ears

mouth

Try to say the names out loud.

Here is Big Bear. Where are his eyes?
Where is Big Bear's nose?
Where are Big Bear's ears?
Where is Big Bear's mouth?

Can you point to your own eyes, nose, ears and mouth?

Say the names of these parts of the body out loud, too.

arms

Can you wave your arms in the air, just like the Bears?

hands

Hold up your hands. What do you use your hands for?

legs

Point to your legs. What do you do with your legs?

feet

Each bear has two feet. How many feet do you have?

tummy

Where is your tummy? Can you find your tummy button?

bottom

Where is your bottom? Can you bounce on your bottom?

Here is a rhyme about parts of the body.
Say the rhyme out loud and do what the words say.
Do you know the names of any other parts of the body?

Hands clap,
Legs jump,
Arms wave,
Feet thump.

Ears listen,
Eyes twinkle,
Mouths smile,
Noses wrinkle.

Heads nod,
Tummies wriggle,
Can you make
Your bottom wiggle?

The Bears are moving in different ways.
Big Bear is walking on tiptoe.
Brown Bear is bouncing on a chair.
Tiny Bear is crawling along the floor.

Can you move like the Bears?

Yellow Bear and Black Bear
are climbing on a chair.
Some of the Bears
are rolling on the rug.

The Bears are going home for tea.
Yellow Bear and Small Bear are walking.
Black Bear and Panda Bear are running.

Can you hop like Brown Bear?
Which bear is jumping?
And who is skipping?

The Bears are having fun.
These bears are going **up** and **down** the stairs.

up

down

Point to the bears which are going up the stairs.
How many bears are going down the stairs?

over

under

These bears are playing games.
Orange Bear is jumping **over** Black Bear.
Tiny Bear is crawling **under** Grey Bear.

behind

beside

in front of

These bears are in the park.
Big Bear is **behind** the tree.
Yellow Bear is **beside** the tree.
Panda Bear is asleep **in front of** the tree.

Here are White Bear and
Orange Bear.
They are going for a walk.
You can see them
from the **front**.

back

front

Now they have turned round.
You can see them
from the **back**.

The Bears are having fun making different sounds.

laughing

Big Bear is laughing.
Do you laugh
when you are tickled?

White Bear is whispering.
Can you whisper, too?

whispering

Black Bear is kissing Yellow Bear.
Can you make the sound of a kiss?

kissing

singing

These bears are singing.
Do you like singing?
What song do you like best?

White Bear and Panda Bear
are clapping.
Can you clap your hands?

clapping

These Bears are stamping.
Can you stamp your feet?

stamping

splashing

These Bears are splashing in the water.
Do you like splashing?

banging

Bang, bang, bang goes Big Bear on his drum.
Yellow Bear and Panda Bear are joining in.
Can you make a banging sound?
What other sounds can you make?

Tiny Bear's birthday

Tiny Bear is excited.
Today is her birthday.

The Bears have given her
lots of presents.

Tiny Bear wants to play hide and seek in the garden.
She wants to hide first.

Can you see where Tiny Bear is hiding?
The Bears cannot find her.

Grey Bear is angry.

Big Bear is worried.   Small Bear is sad.

But Tiny Bear is quite safe.
Panda Bear finds her hiding behind the flowers.
Did you spot where Tiny Bear was hiding?

The Bears are happy.
They are all together again.

'Come on,' says Big Bear.
'It's time for tea. I'm hungry.'
The other Bears are hungry, too.

Big Bear has made a special birthday cake.
Tiny Bear has two slices.
Do you like eating birthday cake?

The Bears are tired.
It has been an exciting day.

And Tiny Bear is
very, very sleepy.

Bears can come,
Bears can go.
Bears are very nice to know.

Bears are friendly,
Bears are fun.
Bears are kind to everyone.

Goodbye!

Bears are happy,
Bears are glad.
Bears are good and never bad.

Bears can tiptoe,
Bears can creep
Bears can run and jump and leap.

Bears can dance,
Bears can sing.
Bears can do 'most anything!